SEEKING PEACE
THROUGH RECONCILIATION

MANAGING ANGER AND
RESOLVING CONFLICTS

A WORKBOOK COMPANION
FOR GROUP STUDY
PART 1

DONALD E. JONES, PHD

J & A BOOK PUBLISHERS
www.jabookpublishers.com

ISBN-10:1-946368-06-7
ISBN-13:978-1-946368-06-5

DEDICATION

I dedicate this book to my Savior and Lord Jesus Christ. He has been with me every step of my journey upon the Earth, and I so look forward to being in His presence forever and ever.

CONTENTS

ACKNOWLEDGMENTS

I want to thank my wonderful and gracious wife Carol who has supported me in this ministry with sacrifice, enthusiasm, encouragement, and accountability. Most of all, she has been a constant blessing because of her willingness to listen. I was always sharing with her the truths God had been teaching me as I studied His word and wrote this book. It consumed many hours. Thank you, Carol, and I deeply love you.

I want to thank my son Gregory R. Jones for volunteering to be the primary editor of this important book. Without his time and effort in painstakingly and meticulously going over every word and every sentence checking and rechecking the sentence structure and grammar, I would not have been able to complete it. Thank you for your ministry to me. I love you my son.

I want to thank my other children, Krista, Matt, and Kara for their love for Christ and His Word and their willingness to live for Him. I love you all.

Introduction

This workbook is designed to aid in the comprehension and application of the truths from the Scriptures which are found in the book of the same name. It has a question and answer format because asking questions was a powerful teaching method that the Lord used to reveal God's divine truth. Jesus asked over one hundred and thirty questions as He instructed the people of God and others. These are only the recorded ones. We can only speculate as to how many questions He might have actually asked. The Lord used His questioning techniques to prompt His listeners to focus, understand, analyze, evaluate, and apply the principles He was proclaiming to them. The same has been done in this workbook.

In Mark chapter 4, after a time of teaching and preaching, Jesus and His disciples travel across the Sea of Galilee on a boat. During their journey, Jesus fell asleep in the stern of the vessel. Suddenly, a huge storm arose and the waves of the sea were beating against the sides of the boat frightening the disciples. Water began to fill the boat and the disciples rushed to waken the Lord. In verse 38, Mark records, "He himself was in the stern, asleep on the cushion, and they woke him up, and told him, 'Teacher, don't you care that we are dying?'" They were deeply afraid for their lives though the God who created the sea and the storm was lying in their boat.

When Jesus awoke, he commanded the storm to be still, and it instantaneously ceased. All became calm. Then, Jesus took this opportunity to ask them a question. In verse 40, Mark writes, "He said to them, 'Why are you so afraid? How is it that you have no faith?'" A demonstration of a strong faith would have been complete confidence in the Lord's protection. He would have known the storm was coming and had decided what He would do about it. His slumber should have brought confidence not fear. Yet, even after being rebuked by the Lord, they became even more fearful because He was able to calm the storm. It frightened them more to see the storm stop than for it to continue. On numerous occasions Jesus questioned their faith and verified His deity. As Jesus used questions, so shall we. May these questions help you focus, understand, analyze, evaluate, and apply these biblical principles.

Chapter 1

Put Anger Away

The biggest hindrance in the reconciliation process will come from our anger. This raging emotion can rear its ugly head during every step in the restoration of a relationship and must be dealt with.

In the section, "A Typical Scenario," the author describes an angry exchange between two brothers over a family reunion which will require a reconciliation.

What is the scenario about?

What did the conflict concern?

What was the relationship between the parties?

Have you had a similar experience?

In the section, "A Scriptural Principle" the author presents an important biblical principle in the process of reconciliation which concerns eliminating our anger.

How would you express this principle in your own words?

How would you rewrite this principle to make it even more personal to your life (using your name and situation)?

Why do you think this principle might be important in your life right now?

How would you rate yourself on the percentage of times you followed this principle in the past when you did something wrong in a relationship?

Directions: Put a horizontal mark and your name where you see yourself on the percentage line.

0%   25%   50%   75%   100%

In the section, "A Biblical Explanation," the author explains the reasons why we must eliminate our anger whenever it arises and how to do it.

According to Ephesians 4:31 and Colossians 3:8, what are Christians supposed to do with their anger?

According to Psalm 37:8, what is the eventual result of all expressions of anger?

According to Ephesians 4:26, are angry feelings sinful? Why or why not?

According to Psalm 4:4, what is the first step in the process of eliminating anger?

What are the second and third steps in removing anger?

In what ways might these truths impact your relationships?

In the section, "An Ancient Portrait," the author provides a unique portrayal of the relationship between Saul and David and how it went awry.

What had David done to make Saul have such affection for him?

What suddenly caused Saul to become so angry at David?

What did Saul do with his anger that caused it to become even more intense?

How did Saul involve his two daughters and son in his evil schemes to kill David?

What were some of David righteous responses as he was running from Saul?

Have you ever been in any situation comparable to Saul's jealousy or David's innocence? How was it different? How was it the same?

In the section, "A Modern Anecdote," the author discusses a situation involving a widowed senior, his neighbor, and a barking dog which needed reconciliation.

Why was the widowed senior so angry with his neighbor?

What were some of the ways the widowed senior attempted to cope with the barking dog?

Rather than confront the neighbor, what did the senior do?

What finally happened that made him come to his senses?

How should God's Word be involved in this situation?

Based on the truths learned in this chapter, what would you do if you were the widowed senior annoyed by the barking dog or the neighbor unaffected by the noisy animal?

In the section, "A Personal Response," the author provides a model you may use for prayer if you find it necessary after discovering the truths in this chapter.

Are you presently in a relationship where you have sinned against another and have not asked God for forgiveness? If not, is there one from the past that still needs this prayer to be prayed?

Based on the truths you have just learned, what will you continue doing in your current relationships and what will you do differently?

What additional thoughts would you like to share with the others?

Chapter 2

Cover in Love

When people come into conflicts in relationships, they do not have to argue or quarrel to resolve them. One approach is to cover over the smaller issues in love.

In the section, "A Typical Scenario," the author describes an angry rant by a man over his step-daughter's actions which may require a reconciliation.

What is the scenario about?

What did the conflict concern?

What was the relationship between the parties?

Have you had a similar experience?

In the section, "A Scriptural Principle" the author presents an important biblical principle in the process of reconciliation which concerns covering over the smaller issues in love.

How would you express this principle in your own words?

How would you rewrite this principle to make it even more personal to your life (using your name and situation)?

Why do you think this principle might be important in your life right now?

How would you rate yourself on the percentage of times you followed this principle in the past when you did something wrong in a relationship?

Directions: Put a horizontal mark and your name where you see yourself on the percentage line.

0%	25%	50%	75%	100%

In the section, "A Biblical Explanation," the author explains the reasons why we should cover over the smaller issues in love and how to do it.

What is the first step in covering over the small things in love?

According to Proverbs 19:11, when someone sins against us what response brings honor to us?

What is the next step that should be taken if the issues are not as small?

What question can we ask ourselves to help us cover over a smaller sin or annoyance?

According to psalm 37:8, what action should we engage in to completely cover over an issue?

In what ways might these truths impact your relationships?

In the section, "An Ancient Portrait," the author provides an example of Abraham preventing a conflict with his nephew Lot by covering over an issue in love.

What conflict did Abraham anticipate might happen with Lot if he did not take action?

What choice did Abraham give to his nephew in order to avoid the conflict and cover over it in love?

What two reasons did Abraham probably have for covering over the potential conflict in love?

What were the consequences of Lot's selfish choice?

Though his nephew had taken the better land, how did his uncle show him he still loved him?

Have you ever been in a situation comparable to Abraham's prevention or Lot's choice? How was it different? How was it the same?

In the section, "A Modern Anecdote," the author discusses a situation where a husband and wife have become irritated over a variety of smaller issues in their relationship.

Who did the author ask the upset couple to focus on besides themselves and why?

What should we do with the strengths that the other person brings to our relationship?

What can we do with small annoyances or weaknesses of the other person that cannot be changed?

What should we do with the annoyances or weaknesses that can be or should be changed?

What should we do with the differences between us and the other person in the relationship?

Based on the truths learned in this chapter, what would you have done differently if you were the husband or wife?

In the section, "A Personal Response," the author provides a model you may use for prayer if you find it necessary after discovering the truths in this chapter.

Are you presently in a relationship where you have sinned against another and have not asked God for forgiveness? If not, is there one from the past that still needs this prayer to be prayed?

Based on the truths you have just learned, what will you continue doing in your current relationships and what will you do differently?

What additional thoughts would you like to share with the others?

Chapter 3

Resolve in Unity

Another way in which Christians can prevent arguments and quarreling is to proceed to a decision-making process. These are reserved for the more serious irritations, problems, and issues that arise.

In the section, "A Typical Scenario," the author describes an issue between a husband and wife that had not been settled, though the arguing had ended.

What is the scenario about?

What did the conflict concern?

What was the relationship between the parties?

Have you had a similar experience?

In the section, "A Scriptural Principle" the author presents an important biblical principle in the process of reconciliation which concerns a decision-making process for larger issues.

How would you express this principle in your own words?

How would you rewrite this principle to make it even more personal to your life (using your name and situation)?

Why do you think this principle might be important in your life right now?

How would you rate yourself on the percentage of times you followed this principle in the past when you did something wrong in a relationship?

Directions: Put a horizontal mark and your name where you see yourself on the percentage line.

| 0% | 25% | 50% | 75% | 100% |

In the section, "A Biblical Explanation," the author explains the reasons why we should deal with the larger issues in a decision making process and how to do it.

According to Romans 12:11 and 1 Corinthians 1:10, what should be the first two steps in the decision-making process and why?

According to 1 Thessalonians 5:21– 22, how do we actually make the decisions in the process?

According to 1 Corinthians 10:24 and 1 Peter 2:17, what is to be our motivation in the decision-making process?

According to Philippians 2:3–4, what should we be willing to do to find unity in the decision?

According to Proverbs 11:14 and 1 Corinthians 1:10, what should be done if a decision can't be made?

In what ways might these truths impact your relationships?

In the section, "An Ancient Portrait," the author provides an example of a conflict between Paul and Peter.

What was the conflict between Paul and the Judaizers?

How did Paul resolve the conflict with them?

What was the conflict Peter and Paul had?

How did Paul resolve it?

What was Peter's presumed response?

Have you ever been in any situation comparable to Paul's obligation to confront his fellow apostle or Peter's mistaken actions? How was it different? How was it the same?

In the section, "A Modern Anecdote," the author describes a conflict between two spouses over their parents.

Briefly, what did the conflict between the spouses concern?

What was the author's first step in resolving the issue?

What issues needed to be discussed in the decision-making process?

How did the couple resolve the issue?

How did the couple share it with their respective parents?

Based on the truths learned in this chapter, what would you have done differently if you were the husband or the wife with the different kind of parents?

In the section, "A Personal Response," the author provides a model you may use for prayer if you find it necessary after discovering the truths in this chapter.

Are you presently in a relationship where you have sinned against another and have not asked God for forgiveness? If not, is there one from the past that still needs this prayer to be prayed?

Based on the truths you have just learned, what will you continue doing in your current relationships and what will you do differently?

What additional thoughts would you like to share with the others?

Chapter 4

Utilize a Mediator

At times, believers will not be able to resolve a conflict or reconcile their relationship by themselves. When this occurs, they should seek a mediator.

In the section, "A Typical Scenario," the author describes a brother's issue with his sister that needed a mediator.

What is the scenario about?

What did the conflict concern?

What was the relationship between the parties?

Have you had a similar experience?

In the section, "A Scriptural Principle" the author presents an important biblical principle in the process of reconciliation which concerns the seeking of a mediator.

How would you express this principle in your own words?

How would you rewrite this principle to make it even more personal to your life (using your name and situation)?

Why do you think this principle might be important in your life right now?

How would you rate yourself on the percentage of times you followed this principle in the past when you did something wrong in a relationship?

Directions: Put a horizontal mark and your name where you see yourself on the percentage line.

0%	25%	50%	75%	100%

In the section, "A Biblical Explanation," the author explains the reasons why we should utilize a mediator if a conflict cannot be resolved and how to select one.

According to Galatians 6:1 and 1 Corinthians 6:5, what must we do if we are unable to reconcile with another?

What are some reasons why we may not be able to reconcile and need help?

What are the first four qualifications for choosing a mediator and why are they important?

What are the fifth and sixth qualifications that a mediator should possess and why are they important?

Where are three groups Christians can find mediators?

In what ways might these truths impact your relationships?

In the section, "An Ancient Portrait," the author provides an example of Paul mediating a reconciliation between a master and his runaway slave.

Why did Paul have to mediate a conflict between Onesimus and Philemon?

Why was Paul the perfect mediator for this issue?

What are some reasons Paul gave to Philemon to reconcile with Onesimus?

How did Paul want to handle the slave's possible theft?

How did Paul subtlety hold Philemon accountable for doing "the right thing"?

Have you ever been in a situation comparable to Philemon's betrayal, Onesimus' difficulty, or Paul's mediation? How was it different? How was it the same?

In the section, "A Modern Anecdote," the author describes a ministry conflict between an older and younger woman.

Why did the pastor put the two women together?

What different strengths did the two women bring to the relationship and ministry?

What weaknesses did each have which were manifested in their ministry?

What differences did the women bring to their relationship?

How did the two decide to utilize their strengths, support their weaknesses, and accept their differences?

Based on the truths learned in this chapter, what would you have done differently if you were the older, experienced woman or the younger, energetic woman?

In the section, "A Personal Response," the author provides a model you may use for prayer if you find it necessary after discovering the truths in this chapter.

Are you presently in a relationship where you have sinned against another and have not asked God for forgiveness? If not, is there one from the past that still needs this prayer to be prayed?

Based on the truths you have just learned, what will you continue doing in your current relationships and what will you do differently?

What additional thoughts would you like to share with the others?

Conclusion

As we conclude this book, I would like to leave us with some final thoughts about our God of reconciliation and what His Son did on the cross for us. First, if we understand the full extent of what was wrought for us on that cursed tree in order to make peace with us, it will become so much easier to do the same thing for others. Second, if you read this entire book and realized that you do not understand salvation or have never received Christ as Lord and Savior, then I would like to provide that opportunity. Please do not skip this section; it may be the most important in your life.

From all outward appearances, humans seem "good" and attempt to live decent lives. This is man's concept of himself. This is not God's concept. The Almighty's view is that people all over the world and throughout the ages sin, sin, and sin again (Romans 3:23). This is a terrible and utterly destructive condition. Yet, they have ramifications that are far worse. These sins condemn us to everlasting divine retribution.

Though described briefly in the Old Testament, the Lord Jesus Christ clearly announced and proclaimed the future punishment to come. Contrary to popular belief, Jesus did not only speak of love, grace, and mercy, He also spoke of the coming judgment for sin. He declared that the judgment of sin would be everlasting punishment in a place He called "Hell." The Lord portrayed this place as an eternal inferno (Matthew 18:8) where there would be the weeping (from the sorrow) and gnashing of teeth (from the agony and anguish of suffering) continually into eternity (Matthew 8:12; 13:42, 50; 22:13; 24:51; 25:30; Luke 13:28).

Why must people face this horrific punishment? Though God is a God of love, grace, and mercy, He is also a God of great holiness, righteousness, and justice (Psalm 89:14,18). These attributes are just as much a part of His divine nature as His love, grace, and mercy. You have broken God's law as we all have and the penalty must be paid. This began with the first man Adam (Genesis 3:1-7). When this occurred, His love, grace, and mercy surfaced and a provision was made. Someone else would have to take man's place and pay the penalty. Someone who had never transgressed Him, who would never deserve punishment, and would fulfill all of God's Laws, would be substituted in man's place. This was the Son of God, Jesus Christ.

As the God-Man, He would pay the penalty for our sins in His death on the cross. Once done, the Lord God made only one provision for people to appropriate what His Son had done on the cross for them. This provision is receiving Jesus Christ as Savior and Lord. Though I cannot possibly share with you this good news in the confines of this book, I would love for you to consider purchasing my book entitled, *Finding The Light: The Kingdom of Heaven and How To Enter It*. It can be found for sale on Amazon.com. It is inexpensive and contains the full gospel message for your consideration. This message is so important and extensive that it cannot adequately be contained in a few pages at the end of a book.

If you are a believer, you must go out into the world and seek peace through reconciliation as God did for us. These principles are to be lived and shared with others. You now have the tools to make your relationships last a lifetime. Go live them out and share them with others!

ABOUT THE AUTHOR

Dr. Donald Jones is currently a Christian Pastoral Counselor with thirty-eight years of experience in the fields of pastoral ministry, public education, and Christian counseling. He carries degrees and certificates from four major universities and from a variety of educational institutions. He has been a professor of Languages and Bible, a television commentator, and a featured speaker at a variety of events and seminars at churches, schools, and other organizations across the United States. He is a member in good standing of several secular and Christian professional organizations. Dr. Jones has been a published author since 1976. For further information view his website at www.donjonesphd.com.

www.ingramcontent.com/pod-product-compliance
Lightning Source LLC
Chambersburg PA
CBHW031618040426
42452CB00006B/582